# KINGDOM, STATE AND
# CIVIL SOCIETY IN AFRICA:
# POLITICAL AND CONCEPTUAL COLLISIONS

Nelson Kasfir

# KINGDOM, STATE AND
# CIVIL SOCIETY IN AFRICA:
# POLITICAL AND CONCEPTUAL COLLISIONS

Carl Schlettwein Lecture 11
Basler Afrika Bibliographien

CARL SCHLETTWEIN
STIFTUNG

The Basler Afrika Bibliographien is part of the Carl Schlettwein Foundation

Cover image: Anniversary parade celebrating the victory over
the socialist Derg-regime in Harrar, Ethiopia (Till Förster 2010)
Editors: Veit Arlt, Till Förster, Anthony Stewart
Layout and typesetting: Tilo Richter

ISBN 978-3-905758-89-4
ISSN 2297-7058

# FOREWORD

It seems to be an old question: What does it mean to be a traditional ruler in contemporary Africa? Unsurprisingly, it was raised in colonial times. Many a colonial officer had to deal with rulers whose allegiance to the colonial state was anything but certain. Labelled as 'traditional', these chiefs and kings effectively drew their power from different sources; as intermediary rulers from the monopoly of power that the state laid claim to, and as heirs of a distant past, built on largely patrimonial regimes. The two domains seemed radically different: a legal-bureaucratic administration on one side versus a political regime apparently rooted in a timeless past. In reality, however, there were parallels between the two domains: First, the institutions of the colonial – and later the postcolonial – state were much weaker than its representatives pretended, and second, the continuity of traditional rule was rarely as self-evident as its rulers claimed. In both fields, domination had to be staged in a manner that convinced the local population of its legitimacy. The sources of legitimacy were different in the two domains – but they always had to be made persuasive by means other than those they officially put forward.

Successful 'traditional rulers' often became savvy political actors who repeatedly re-invented tradition as a useful past that allowed them to legitimize their own position, combining it with elements of legal-bureaucratic domination. This practice did not change much when African colonies became independent states around 1960. De facto, it is often difficult if not impossible to draw a clear line between traditional, patrimonial legitimacy and other types that would be classified as 'modern'. The grand dichotomy of traditional versus modern has little explanatory value, and more often than not, is of no help at all. Political actors in Africa make claims to the past and the present when that serves their interests – not because they incarnate one or the other. When, several decades after independence, the repertoire of collective claim-making had been enlarged by civil society organizations and their publics, many traditional rulers embraced these new possibilities, sometimes redefining themselves in these new terms as advocacy groups, non-governmental organizations, or self-help organizations. Their inventiveness and creativity is simply stunning.

This often overwhelmingly complex formation of politics in contemporary Africa is a double challenge for African studies as an interdisciplinary field and also for political science, history, sociology and anthropology, fields that share a broader interest in these processes. First, the study of such processes is an empirical challenge as many actors may mask their knowledge and motives. Traditional rulers rarely have an interest in revealing the constructed, discursive nature of their claims to the past as that could call their legitimacy into question: Their rule must be a 'natural' corollary of their peoples' history. Second, the concepts of political theory that build on and relate to Western history very rarely capture the specificities of these political formations. Is, for instance, a support group of a 'traditional' ruler a civil society organization or not? Is an association of dignitaries that calls itself a government and that has real power in certain fields a state organization or an NGO? The study of African politics often challenges conventional political theory – and within this wider field, so-called traditional rulers are certainly one of the most prominent topics.

In his essay, Nelson Kasfir analyses such a case, the restoration of the *Kabaka*, the king of the Baganda, after Yoweri Museveni became Uganda's President in 1986. Against expectations, the support group succeeded and the *Kabaka* was reinstalled – but his kingdom was not. The *Kabaka* was eventually crowned in 1993, but his kingdom is still not reinstated today. Kasfir studies this remarkable case from two perspectives. One is a thorough, empirically based analysis of the political articulation of interests and the formation of political actors that comes along with it. The second is an examination of whether conventional concepts of Western political theory do justice to the case. Taking this seemingly marginal case as a starting point, he asks big questions of political theory: What kind of organization is the king's government if there is no kingdom to govern? Why is it nonetheless an important factor of Ugandan politics? And not least, what is a government and what is a civil society organization?

Very convincingly, Nelson Kasfir argues that in its applications to Africa, political theory has more to learn from the margins in what is often called the Global South than from the study of mainstream political concepts from the Global North.

Till Förster
University of Basel
November 2017

# KINGDOM, STATE AND
# CIVIL SOCIETY IN AFRICA:
# POLITICAL AND CONCEPTUAL COLLISIONS

Tiny groups of Baganda private citizens formed associations from the moment Yoweri Museveni became President of Uganda in 1986 to persuade the national government to restore the *Kabaka*, their king. Against expectations, they succeeded through a combination of argument, mobilization and negotiations. But, up to now, they have failed to persuade the government to reinstate their kingdom. Their advocacy raises an intriguing question: what sorts of organizations did they create to support their goals? After his coronation in 1993, the new *Kabaka* formed a cabinet, called the Buganda Kingdom Government (BKG) and appointed members mostly from one of those associations to become its ministers.[1] Did that turn that pressure group into a government? Was this group a civil society organization (CSO) before it became the BKG and a government after that? Or, since the national government gave the *Kabaka* only cultural status, could it only ever be a CSO? Yet, since the BKG violates most of the norms built into the Western notion of civil society, could it even be a CSO? These questions raise profound political and conceptual issues involving culture and politics as well as whether Western philosophic notions can explain African behavior.

The original objective, shared by these informal groups, was to bring back from exile Ronald Muwenda Mutebi II, the heir chosen by Frederick Mutesa II the former *Kabaka* (king). Mutesa had fled in 1966 and died in London after Milton Obote's government abolished his kingdom. The group that became the BKG took the lead not only in persuading Uganda's new government to permit Mutebi's return, but through unremitting activism over the next seven years to agree to his coronation in 1993, thus ending a 26-year interruption in a royal line that stretches back centuries. By becoming the BKG, this group enhanced its legitimacy to promote more effectively the interests of the *Kabaka*, and of Baganda in general, as they understood them.

The coronation has so far proved the high point of its advocacy. It has not been able to re-establish the Buganda kingdom as an entity with political authority, law-making powers or fully accepted borders. Its success in re-establishing the monarchy was also incomplete, because the Ugandan constitution declares the *Kabaka* a cultural leader without political authority—unlike his predecessors. While the *Kabaka* could appoint the members of the BKG, it is unclear that the constitution gives them authority to make any political decisions in his name.[2]

Nevertheless, the BKG created many accouterments of government in addition to becoming the cabinet, including regular meetings of a *Lukiiko* (a legislative council), appointments of "traditional" chiefs and envoys to other countries, a flag and an anthem. The BKG also became deeply involved in political issues, publicly advocating land rights, the establishment of the kingdom and the expansion of the authority of the *Kabaka*. Although these questions, mostly involving the central government, were often resolved co-operatively, they sometimes created deep tensions that resulted in serious violence. Many of them resembled the political disputes that had resulted in the central government's military attack on Buganda that led to the abolition of rulership and realm in 1967.

The continuing engagement of the BKG as it pressed for *Kabaka* and kingdom produced both political and conceptual collisions. To begin with, how and why were its members instrumental in persuading the central government to restore the king, but not the kingdom? To what extent did their subsequent efforts to achieve the kingdom within Uganda lead to political tensions? Considering the longstanding heritage represented by the *Kabaka* and his kingdom, is advocacy for their restoration a valiant effort to preserve a living culture or merely to advance a political interest—or both?

The activities of the BKG also pose challenging theoretical questions. What kind of an organization is the BKG? Was it a different type of association before the *Kabaka's* accession to the throne than after it became his cabinet? Was it a government, as its officials insist, or a civil society organization (CSO), as some of its opponents claim? Since both "government" and "civil society" are Western concepts, this last question invites deeper inquiry, asking how and even whether we can translate Western concepts to fit African realities. What gets lost in the translation and what facilitates understanding? In short, the larger conceptual issue I want to reach is what the concepts of government and civil society should mean when applied to African cases. I use the BKG as a vehicle to pursue that discussion.

## POLITICAL COLLISIONS

To unravel the origin and development of the informal group that became the BKG, we need to know who its members were, against whom they competed, what they wanted to do, what rationales they constructed and whether their objectives remained constant or changed. The starting point must be the historic and unrelentingly difficult relationship between Buganda and Uganda. Ali Mazrui put his finger on it long before the current BKG emerged, "... Uganda is an impossible country to govern with the support of the Baganda, but it is also impossible to govern effectively without the support of the Baganda" (1974, 8).[3]

The Buganda Kingdom formed the original core of the British Protectorate of Uganda. Those who could speak in its name acquired privileged positions that they have tried to hold onto ever since, despite challenges from both within and without Buganda. From the colonial period forward, every government of Uganda and the leaders of Buganda began with positive relations that eventually collapsed. This problematic relationship, defined by confrontations over kingship and kingdom, has always been a basic political cleavage in the country. Although at first Museveni was exceptionally popular among Baganda because his soldiers helped overthrow Milton Obote, he did not escape controversies almost identical to those confronting all his predecessors, starting with the colonial governors.

Buganda is Uganda's largest, most populous and most developed region. Its comparative advantages, particularly around the time of independence, led many citizens living in the other three regions to worry that Buganda's leaders would discriminate against them if they became dominant in the central government (Kasfir 1976, 141-142). These non-Baganda regarded the *Kabaka* and his kingdom government as a political contrivance intended to achieve that end. On the other hand, Baganda, especially many of their leaders, have always insisted that the *Kabaka* and kingdom are central to their cultural heritage. When the National Resistance Movement (NRM) government took office, this relationship became especially delicate because its military had started the civil war against the second Obote regime in Buganda and fought it there until the final year.

Although Museveni and most of his top officers in the National Resistance Army (NRA) were Banyankole from the Western region, Baganda became fervent supporters of the NRA rebellion. "There was popular resentment for Obote in Buganda. That made it a perfect choice" (interview, NRA military officer, Kenshunga, 28 November 2003). For a time, the majority of NRA soldiers fighting in Buganda were Baganda (Kasfir 2005, 282-283). Many of them, both civilians and fighters, hoped that victory would mean the restoration of the monarchy. They were encouraged by Mutebi's visit to the war zone in late 1985, one that Museveni had arranged. But when Museveni became president in 1986, he knew that reinstating either king or kingdom would be deeply unpopular everywhere else in the country. And, at the time, many citizens throughout the country were deeply suspicious of Museveni and his new government, in large part because he had seized power by force. Yet in order to rule effectively, he needed to retain support of most Baganda.

## Groups advocating restoration

Three informal groups of Baganda organized to restore the *Kabaka*ship soon after the NRM seized power in January 1986. Besides the BKG, the *Bataka ba Busolya* (the heads of the clans), approximately 50 men, and the *Bazzukulu ba Buganda* (the "Descendants of Buganda"), perhaps 30-40, also formed. None of them had much of a following then. The *Bataka* were better organized, as their customary legitimacy had not been interrupted when Obote ended kingship. Both groups had rural followers but were relatively unimportant national political actors. Then and afterwards, the *Bazzukulu* were also few in number, older, of modest means and poorly educated. They proclaimed their devotion to their ancestral culture, but held no cultural offices and were uncompromising in their demands for the restoration of king and kingdom.

The members of the third group, which became the BKG, were largely urban, young, well-educated lawyers, teachers and landowners. As the *Bataka* and the *Bazzukulu*, they had stayed in Uganda during the violent years of Amin and Obote II. Their elite status stemmed from the 1900 agreement through which the British Protectorate administrators had given title to large amounts of land (called *mailo*) to the *Kabaka* and thousands of his officials in return for their pledge of loyalty to Great Britain. The *Bataka* had lost their cultural rights in these lands, turning them against these chiefs who were new landowners and marking a significant change in Kiganda culture. The ability to borrow against title and command labor on these estates led to an entirely new degree of wealth and inequality among Baganda that resulted in opposition between tenants and landowners. Several members of the BKG were descendants either of the original landowners or other Baganda who had bought their holdings.

All three groups called for the return of Mutebi and all three wanted a federal kingdom over the same area as before, one that exercised its own powers within Uganda—more or less the situation that had existed at independence in 1962. But they differed in how they approached these goals. The *Bataka* needed the *Kabaka* for his role in the clan system that they wanted to promote (Karlström 1999, 216). The members of the BKG were not as wedded to "tradition" as were the *Bataka* and the *Bazzukulu* and were more moderate in their demands on the central government. The BKG "limited their requests" in order to achieve modest goals and then move forward (interview, former BKG official, Kampala 11 November 2014). The BKG's willingness to compromise with Museveni and his officials gave its members a reputation as reliable interlocutors, something the other two groups never achieved.

At first, the prospect to reinstall a king must have seemed improbable. For twenty years there had been none—at best, a "pretender" living in exile, not yet ritually a *Kabaka*. How vital a role did kingship still play in the cultural values of most Baganda? Secular beliefs have gained traction over custom the world over. "The fate of our times," Max Weber lamented, "is characterized by rationalization and intellectualization and, above all, by the 'disenchantment of the world'" (1958 [1919], 155). As a practical matter, Baganda support must also have appeared doubtful. Considering that most Baganda regarded Museveni and the NRM, now the government, as their liberators and knew that the NRM publicly advocated anti-ethnic and anti-traditional values, how many of them would support an abashedly ethnic campaign? Furthermore, outspoken Baganda opinion leaders who had joined the NRA rejected a return to "tradition". Soon after taking power, the NRM itself had insisted it "has never promised to restore monarchs" (*New Vision*, 22 July 1986, quoted in Karlström 1999, 273). Museveni declared in a public speech "that he did not go to the bush to fight for 'tribal chiefs'" (Mayiga 2009, 28).

Nevertheless, there was clearly cultural sentiment for restoration, even if, during the early days, no one knew how deeply felt. Politically, that meant the absence of a *Kabaka* created an opportunity to restructure the institution to make it more acceptable to supporters and opponents. If the kingship were redefined as cultural rather than political, it would be less threatening to the new NRM government, uncertain of its support throughout the country.

The BKG was intent on making the cultural argument the basis for its rationale for restoration: "Culturally, the

*Kabaka* is the embodiment of our identity—everything, including clan identity, leads to it" (interview, BKG official, Kampala, 21 May 2010). "'... there is no other institution or authority which can credibly claim to speak for Buganda or for the Baganda as a single, indivisible and intergenerational native African nation'" (David Mpanga, a BKG Minister, quoted in Nsibambi 2014, 27). But, accepting that the *Kabaka* was clearly a cultural figure left an important question conveniently overlooked for the time being. Didn't his cultural status entail the highest political position that his forefathers had occupied in years past? And further, as his promoters who were to become members of the BKG pointed out, in the old days, the *Kabaka* had appointed officials to carry out his orders. "The *Katikkiro* [Prime Minister] and chiefs provide services—it's part of our history, it's part of our culture" (interview, BKG senior official, Kampala, 8 June 2010). Is the BKG merely as cultural as the *Kabaka*?

## Lobbying led to kingship

Soon after Museveni became President, the heads of two clans and a lawyer met him to encourage him to permit Mutebi to come home (interview with a person at the meeting, Kampala, 11 November 2014). The clan heads argued that Baganda were eager to have their *Kabaka* again and that he performed important rites in the life of ordinary people, for example, establishing heirs. They assured Museveni his return would not cause problems. When Museveni insisted Mutebi could not come back as *Kabaka*, they asked if he could return as *Ssabataka* (the head of all the clans). Mutebi had already passed through the rituals for this cultural position during his visit in 1971 for his father's burial. Museveni consented and in August 1986, Andrew Lwanga, an NRA officer close to Museveni, met Mutebi at the Kenyan border and drove him to Kampala for a visit (Mayiga 2009, 30).[4] Mutebi was nervous about his safety during this visit, but came home for good in November 1986 (Oloka-Onyango 1997, 177). Still, he felt that "the future did not seem certain" (Mayiga 2009, 30).

An unofficial group soon formed to advise Mutebi (Mayiga 2009, 30-31). It consisted of a mix of men originally officials of his father joined by younger professionals. The latter eventually eclipsed the former and went on to join the BKG. "We had small meetings of about 12.... People were scared [of the NRM's anti-ethnic stance]" (interview, former BKG official, Kampala, 11 November 2014). None of them were paid. They organized the famous football competition among clans to demonstrate the esteem Baganda felt for Mutebi (Mayiga 2009, 35). In June 1991, Mutebi enlarged this advisory group to 18, adding younger members and letting some of the holdovers from his father's cabinet go, as well as some clan heads. "The moderate royalists ... moved to marginalize the Bataka radicals ...." (Karlström 1999, 231). This group was called the *Ssabataka*'s Supreme Council (SSC). One consequence was to distance the *Bataka* and *Bazzukulu* from Mutebi. His preference for the young professionals increased their legitimacy to speak for him.[5] However, the other two groups also had supporters and on occasion effectively criticized the SSC and later the BKG.

Upon its formation, the SSC took the precaution of informing Museveni of their intentions. It solicited Baganda opinions to prepare its proposal for the draft that eventually became the 1995 constitution. Its members also searched for revenue to sustain its activities and Mutebi's expenses (Mayiga 2009, 44-45). In its constitutional submission the SSC took a prudent position by recommending that kings be reinstated, but not as political actors (Mayiga 2009, 51-53). It also urged the adoption of a federal regime in Buganda and recommitment to *mailo* land tenure. In contrast, the *Bataka* and *Bazzukulu* called for an immediate return to the independence constitution that had recognized the Buganda Kingdom Government as a fully federal body with the power to make laws, raise revenue and judge cases (Karlström 1999, 229-230).

The SSC gained greater trust from the NRM government by participating in the constitutional process. That gave it an opening to become the negotiating partner with the national government for the return of the properties (*ebyaffe*) confiscated by the Obote government in 1967 following its military scuffle with Buganda. Obote had incurred deep hostility from most Baganda, by giving the Buganda Parliament building (the *Bulange*) and the *Kabaka's* palace (the *Lubiri*) to his army. Surprisingly, the NRA also chose to occupy these buildings after it defeated the military successor to the second Obote government. The BKG knew it would solidify its position among most Baganda by negotiating the return of these properties as well as others belonging to the Buganda government and the *Kabaka*.

If Museveni handed the properties back, however, he could expect to incur resentment in the rest of the country (Mayiga 2009, 102). In addition, there would be opposition from many of his generals in the NRA, who felt (as did the President) that Buganda was a large part of the problems that had led to the cycle of coups and violence in past years. But Museveni was also looking ahead to secure the NRM's position as the government in the new constitution that would soon be debated. On balance, he felt his best political strategy was to return at least some of these properties.[6] Four members of the SSC met him privately, probably in early 1992, cautiously choosing to "limit their requests," yet successfully resisting his proposal that the central government hold the *Bulange* for five more years (interview with person at this meeting, Kampala, 11 November 2014). Significantly, they based their rationale for immediate return of the *Bulange* on cultural grounds—the previous *Kabaka* had blessed the signs of the clans in the building.[7] Museveni also agreed at this meeting to negotiate the return of the 350 square mile personal estates of the *Kabaka*, realizing that it would endow the king and the BKG with an important source of revenue.

Nevertheless, Museveni still had to overcome significant opposition in the NRA and the National Resistance Council (NRC, then the national legislature). He did not have an easy time with his generals. In the Army Council meeting in April 1992, "we told him [Mr. Museveni] not to return these obsolete institutions and he did not listen to us. He begged, he pleaded, he went on his knees and the army grudgingly accepted to return these things...." (Major General Kahinda Otafiire in *Monitor*, 10 September 2009). Negotiators from the SSC and the central government had a difficult time deciding which properties to return (Nsibambi 2014, 68). The SSC put pressure on the government by holding public processions that ended in rallies at Parliament (Mayiga 2009, 91). In April 1993, Museveni persuaded the NRC to agree to return the most symbolic of the properties confiscated in 1967. The decision greatly increased the SSC's claim to represent Baganda interests.

As it was negotiating the return of royal properties (*ebyaffe*, literally "our things"), the SSC continued to develop its parallel track, the restoration of the *Kabaka*. In July 1992, it began to plan its path to crown Mutebi (Mayiga 2009, 109-110). With negotiations for the return of properties complete by the beginning of March 1993, the SSC formally chose Mutebi to become the next *Kabaka* (Mayiga 2009, 110).[8] Both the *Bataka* and the *Bazzukulu* were opposing a coronation, insisting that it made no sense to crown a *Kabaka* until he could have a kingdom, something missing from the draft constitution (Karlström 1999, 240-241). The SSC recognized that it had to support kings throughout the country, if it were to have its own. In July 1993, the NRC passed an amendment to the 1967 Constitution permitting any cultural group to choose a "traditional" ruler (Nsibambi 2014, 69-70). However, the amendment prohibited any such ruler from participating in politics. Having committed itself earlier to a cultural position for the *Kabaka*, the BKG had no choice but to go along.

The coronation on 31 July 1993 represents the epitome of BKG efforts to lobby the government as sponsor for Baganda interests. It meant the BKG, as it now became, was widely understood to speak for the *Kabaka* and the interests of Baganda. Its authority, however, was challenged as new issues arose in which it was either unable to persuade the central government or took pragmatic positions that were repudiated by the Baganda public. Discovering the limits of perceived cultural authority has been a daunting challenge over the turbulence of political and cultural changes during the past 125 years, particularly since the abolition of the kingdom.

In their first steps after the coronation, the SSC turned itself into the BKG by creating the symbols of political authority. Its leaders intended to signal its different audiences that they wanted to be understood to be a government. The decisions they made exposed the inconsistency between adherence to culture and current administrative practice. They organized a cabinet that included several ministries unknown to pre-colonial Kiganda culture (for a list, see Mayiga 2009, 154-167). The new *Lukiiko*, whose members were appointed by the *Kabaka*, assembled immediately after the coronation in the (just returned) *Bulange* (Englebert 2002, 349). Over the next few years despite the prohibition on any local administration by cultural leaders in the 1995 Constitution, the *Kabaka* and the BKG resurrected the chiefship hierarchy and chose *ssaza* (county), *gombolola* (subcountry) and *miluka* (parish) chiefs, mirroring *Kabakas* in the colonial and early post-independence regimes (Englebert 2002, 350-351). At the same time, the BKG modeled itself on contemporary governments by choosing a flag, an anthem and ambassadors to various foreign countries. Unlike those governments, however, it could not afford to pay any of its officials.

The coronation set the scene for new political conflicts between the BKG and the central government. The next step as the BKG saw it was to create a federal kingdom. From Museveni's perspective, there was no next step. "The point all along after the restoration of the *Kabaka*," a BKG official insisted, "was to advocate for self-determination for the kingdom, so that it retains its cultural autonomy" (interview, Kampala, 10 November 2014). Often, the BKG and Museveni found compromises to solve particular issues. But ordinary Baganda rejected some of these settlements, even questioning the fundamental demand for a kingdom (Karlström 1999, 453). The differences among all participants soon led to political collisions, including the most violent clashes other than the armed rebellions that have occurred during Museveni's long rule.

### Defensive advocacy
### following the coronation

Five complicated issues over the two decades since the coronation illustrate the BKG's problems in defending Baganda interests. Most led either to rejection by the central government or compromise with the government subsequently rejected by ordinary Baganda. These issues involved the BKG's efforts to consolidate the political kingdom, land issues and fending off a daring effort by Museveni to promote new cultural heads within Buganda. The last led to riots in September 2009 that caused a political collision between Baganda and national leaders seeming to show Museveni's cultural policy had not resolved their basic confrontation any better than had past regimes. In 2013, the central government's initiative to return additional Baganda properties somewhat calmed the waters.

The first issue involved the BKG's defense of Baganda interests, as it understood them, in the Constituent Assembly (CA) that passed the 1995 Constitution. At that moment, the BKG regarded the NRM as its ally. The BKG worked with Baganda delegates in the CA to extend the "no-party" system that protected the NRM government from competition by other parties in return for the NRM's support in entrenching the cultural kingship (Regan 1995, 180; Doornbos and Mwesigye 1995, 62). But the BKG secured only one other important constitutional policy for which it had lobbied — guaranteeing mailo land tenure.[9] It failed to achieve federalism in place of the current decentralized local government. Instead, the CA voted a "Charter of Co-operation" that included all the districts of Buganda, but left administration in the hands of those districts rather than in a Buganda government.[10] In addition, the BKG was unable to persuade enough delegates to return responsibility for the "9,000 square miles" of public land to a Buganda Land Board.[11] "There emerged a high feeling of betrayal .... in Buganda" (Mayiga 2009, 65).

Only a few years later, the central government created a Constitutional Review Commission (CRC), giving the BKG a new prospect for advancing its objectives. The experience demonstrated the narrow limits for change between the central government intent on keeping power and those Baganda intent on promoting fidelity to cultural norms. The BKG persuaded the CRC to adopt a countrywide federal structure, giving a Buganda Land Board control of the 9,000 square miles and keeping Kampala, the capital city within Buganda (Mayiga 2009, 223-226). But the Cabinet opposed returning management of the 9,000 square miles and including Kampala (Mayiga 2009, 227). Museveni was willing to negotiate over regional government with the BKG. The talks broke down but eventually reconvened, leading to a compromise to create a regional assembly with a specific list of functions and consisting of nominees by the cultural head and directly elected members, including a directly elected prime minister (Mayiga 2009, 244-253). This arrangement moved regional government toward federalism, but left it within the decentralization policy, which meant the central government kept control. Furthermore, determination of the regional authority's right to raise revenue was postponed (Nsibambi 2014, 77-78). Museveni also compromised by symbolically including Kampala in Buganda, while keeping control over its management.

The BKG believed it had triumphed, but discovered it had misjudged its constituents. Claiming superior knowledge of traditional customs, the *Bazzukulu* and the *Bataka*, now joined by the *Abamasaza* (the county chiefs, ironically those selected by the *Kabaka*) declared that an elected prime minister would violate Kiganda culture by depriving the *Kabaka* of his age-old right to appoint his *Katikkiro* (prime minister) (Mayiga 2009, 386-393).

That might result in a non-Muganda prime minister! Completely unforeseen, public opinion in newspapers and on radio compelled the *Kabaka* to discard this settlement and even change his ministers. Nevertheless, Parliament, with a majority of NRM MPs, put the compromise settlement into the amended constitution. The BKG was not only humiliated, but ordinary Baganda saw it as allying with their "enemy". Later, a senior BKG official bowed to the popular understanding of this cultural belief, saying, "an elected *Katikkiro* could not be the custodian of culture and the principal advisor to the king" (interview, Kampala, 8 June 2010).

Rights in land between tenants and landlords formed the third issue. The government passed a land act in 1998 and another in 2010. Both increased protection for tenants, while also confirming mailo land tenure. The BKG revealed its class position by championing landowners, while also paying lip service to peasants tilling the land. "The intent [of the land acts] is to weaken the landed; that's the idea behind all land reform" (interview, senior BKG official, Kampala, 8 June 2010). Again, the BKG opposed the central government's refusal to return the 9,000 square miles, this time on the grounds that it did not give "control over land to Buganda as an entity" (Mayiga 2009, 76). Its position was not simply symbolic. It hoped that a Buganda Land Board would prevent corrupt district land boards making deals with wealthy individuals, particularly those who were not Baganda. It also worried about Museveni's penchant for enticing foreign investors by personally giving them choice parcels of land "without consulting the owners" (interview, BKG senior official, Kampala, 8 June 2010).

BKG officials mobilized opinion to prevent MPs from passing the 1998 Act. They "engaged MPs and wrote letters to the press" (interview, BKG official, Kampala, 10 November 2014). After it passed, the *Lukiiko* "resolved that there will be no merry making to mark *Kabaka* Ronald Mutebi II's 5th coronation anniversary, because Buganda had lost out on the land law" (*Monitor*, 1 August 1998). The BKG stressed its commitment to Buganda's cultural traditions. It probably had a hand in organizing a gathering that "will spend the night invoking the gods. The ceremony is part of the many, to mourn...." (*New Vision*, 1 August 1998).

Later, during the years of debate before the 2010 Land Act was passed, the BKG called attention to problems they thought the new bill would cause. They "testified before parliamentary committees and negotiated with Omara Atubo, the Lands Minister to try to get certain clauses removed" (interview BKG official, Kampala, 10 November 2014). Lawyers in the BKG sent memos to MPs arguing defects in the bill. "If you compare the first and last drafts of the Land bill, you will see how much influence our efforts had" (interview BKG official, Kampala, 10 November 2014). The Central Broadcasting Service (CBS) attacked it. In 2008, the BKG also organized the Central Civic Education Committee to give speeches against the bill throughout Buganda. The political temperature shot up when the central government detained the committee members (Mayiga 2009, 403-414). Museveni warned the kings to avoid "politicking over land" (*New Vision*, 11 February 2008).

After succeeding in amending the constitution, Museveni tried a more radical ploy to counter the political ambitions of the BKG. To weaken the *Kabaka*, he encouraged the emergence of other cultural heads in Buganda. He took advantage of Buganda's pre-colonial history of conquering other ethnic groups and then absorbing them. These groups had become Baganda without forgetting their past identities. Museveni used his patronage to elevate these leaders informally, despite their slim to nonexistent claims to kingship. He even attended rituals through which they claimed to rule. Naturally, the BKG was horrified by this gambit and responded by organizing the *Kabaka's* visits to the suddenly disputed parts of his "realm", even if the realm had no existence in the Constitution, other than as the Charter of Co-operation that the *Kabaka* and the BKG had rejected. In 2008 and 2009, the police stopped these efforts to reinforce the *Kabaka's* authority at the borders of the districts that had now become the "boundaries" for the cultural dominions of the new, although not yet authorized, "traditional" upstarts.

Both Museveni and the BKG were shocked when the 2009 blockade erupted in the worst urban riots of the NRM regime. The police stopped the *Katikkiro* from entering Kayunga District to check arrangements for the *Kabaka's* tour the next day, claiming they could not protect him. As soon as word got back to Kampala, riots broke out there and soon in other urban areas in Buganda Region. The central government claimed the riots were planned, the BKG said they were spontaneous. Museveni closed CBS. Now he "clarified" that culture really meant only "to deal with our languages and customs that are not well addressed by the modern institutions" (Museveni 2009, 5).

A hasty meeting between the President and the *Kabaka* did little to allay distrust. The Cabinet produced a harsh Traditional Leaders Bill intended to remove any possibility for political action by a king. It passed, but only after the most draconian clauses had been removed. Still, it prompted a former BKG official to recognize the obvious, " Museveni doesn't really believe in the culture of kings" (interview, Kampala, 11 November 2014). This episode was the most serious political collision during Museveni's regime.

Perhaps intending to resurrect the BKG as his channel to resolve problems with Baganda interests, Museveni suddenly offered in 2013 to give back more of the Buganda properties that Obote had confiscated in 1967. "It came out of the blue" (interview, BKG official, Kampala, 6 November 2014). For over twenty years, the BKG had been demanding the return of all its properties. The 1995 constitution and the 1993 Traditional Rulers statute had obligated the central government to return them (*Monitor*, 25 July 2008). Instead, the government had separated culture from the political in yet another way by agreeing to give back properties associated with the king, but not those associated with the kingdom, such as offices of chiefs (*Monitor*, 29 May 2007).

Not only did the 2013 Memorandum of Understanding (MoU) list 213 additional properties for return, including administrative offices, it also offered to reimburse the unpaid rent since 1993 and gave assurances it would not stop the *Kabaka* from traveling anywhere within Buganda Region (interview with a BKG official, Kampala, 6 November 2014). However, Museveni had not forgotten the other supposed cultural leaders he had discovered a few years earlier. The memorandum adds, "the *Kabaka* shall respect the cultural norms of other related ethnic communities located in Buganda such as the Banyala and Baruli, and leave to them land where the former administrative units were situated ...." (quoted in *Observer* (Kampala), 10 June 2014). In the eyes of the BKG, "the MoU changed the tone of their relationship from confrontational to negotiable" (BKG official, interview, Kampala, 6 November 2014).

## CONCEPTUAL COLLISIONS

How shall we account for the anomalous status of the BKG? Is it part of political society or civil society? Should we treat it as a government or as a CSO? Or neither? Just asking the question is culturally and politically explosive. Labeling it one or the other means taking sides in the Ugandan debate. As a BKG official told me, when central government ministers dismiss the BKG as "just an NGO," they intentionally denigrate our defense of Kiganda culture (interview, Kampala, 10 November 2014). Nevertheless, posing this question is not a scholastic exercise. Using Western concepts to explore African organizations is problematic. There is a double problem here. First, there is the question of what kind of an organization the BKG is; and second, there is the lack of fit when notions developed from Western experience are applied to African cases. The conceptual pay-off lies in using this unusual organization to explore how these concepts apply in African conditions.

## Is the BKG a government?

Since BKG officials insist they are directing a government and invest considerable energy, time and money into what appear to be governmental activities, we should consider their claim seriously. If appearances are sufficient, the BKG must have become a government after the coronation. The *Kabaka* and BKG leaders created an impressive array of offices that typically characterize governments. And, the central government accepted them, despite the constitutional prohibition. In Oloka-Onyango's insouciant aside: "... President Museveni attended the opening of the restored *Lukiiko* and did not bat an eyelid on being introduced to the ministers and other officials of the Buganda government" (1997, 182). While insisting that kings hold only cultural offices, the central government has tolerated their creation of ministers, chiefs and various seemingly governmental activities throughout Uganda. However, since almost all these officials are volunteers, none of them, including the BKG, have a salaried bureaucracy unlike most contemporary governments.

To make the argument for government in constitutional terms, Mayiga, an adroit lawyer, seizes on the provision that "'the institution of traditional leader or cultural leader shall be a corporation sole with perpetual succession....'" (Art. 246(3)(a)) to claim, "it was arguable that the *Kabaka* could establish organs or systems to sustain this office, which one could characterize as a 'government', ultimately" (2009, 70, see also 154). The tentative character of his formulation suggests he realizes this clause protects the inheritance of kingship (as opposed to making it available for reassignment on the death of a king) and cannot in itself be the basis for establishing an executive government. In any case, his point is significantly undermined by the constitutional provision that "a traditional leader or cultural leader shall not have or exercise any administrative, legislative or executive powers of Government or local government" (Art. 246(3)(f)). And worse, the BKG was forced to disavow the regional tier when public opinion determined that accepting an elected *Katikkiro* would violate culture.[12] Had the regional tier been implemented, the BKG would have had a much stronger case that it possessed legal status.

Is it a government, if it does not govern? Unquestionably, the BKG intends to govern. But that is insufficient to qualify it as part of political society, for unlike political parties it does not have the legal capacity to become a government. The critical test of government, as Weber reminds us, is whether citizens comply with its commands "through [its] readiness to resort to physical force, including normally force of arms" (1978 [1922], 901). While many Baganda may justify following BKG decisions as cultural obligations, they obey Ugandan laws because the police and courts enforce them.

As well, the question of territorial boundaries is confused. Weber insists, "the territory must at any time be in some way determinable ...." (1978 [1922], 902). As a cultural leader only, the *Kabaka* would appear to have followers, but not a territory.[13] Yet, the constitution recognizes geographic boundaries for Buganda Region. Furthermore, the central government implicitly recognized that Buganda has boundaries (not just its districts) when it tried to stop the *Kabaka* from visiting places that it claimed were no longer part of his kingdom.

Of course, the BKG case for government rests on an additional foundation, that its offices are rooted in its age-old culture. Kiganda culture clearly entailed government throughout its history as an independent nation, and, although to a more constricted degree, during the Protectorate and first years of independence. Several writers argue that the BKG's custody of custom provides a rationale for considering it a government. Mayiga, for example, insists that by calling a traditional leader an "institution" rather than just referring to a king as a person imports the customs that had existed before abolition (2009, 154-55).[14] Englebert puts forward a broader rationale, contending that the BKG is part of "a resurgence of pre-colonial political institutions", although conceding that it has produced only a "quasi-state institution" so far (2002, 345, 347). Goodfellow and Lindemann also consider the BKG a "traditional authority," but one that resulted in "discordant institutional multiplicity" when it was introduced into government (2013, 9, 20-22).[15]

In all three cases, however, the insuperable difficulty with establishing the BKG as a contemporary government on the basis of former cultural practices is that the meaning of government has changed. The use of "traditional authority" smuggles in the idea that culture is static. In the pre-colonial period, the most important BKG officials received the compliance of lesser chiefs and ordinary inhabitants because they were their patrons and because they had broad capacity to punish. Although stripped of the harshest of those powers during the Protectorate, chiefs still had wide-ranging legal authority to give orders and judge whether they were followed; those who failed to obey faced arrest. A contemporary cultural rationale could certainly be constructed, but it would have to be a new endeavor.

If we pay even cursory attention to the contemporary BKG in comparison to its predecessors, we find two kinds of cultural changes. First, many pre-colonial customs involving governance are no longer followed. Second, novel official positions and policies have been grafted onto this cultural revival. The pre-colonial kingdom did not have defined territorial boundaries. If we accept that the current one does, then we have to account for the basis of BKG's governance over the substantial population, perhaps one-third, in Buganda Region that are not Baganda. Would a kingdom based on cultural loyalty have any basis to command their obedience? This issue is complicated by the constitutional prohibition of compulsory allegiance to a traditional leader (Art. 246(3)(d)). How then could a government justified on the basis of culture govern them?

In addition, many of today's BKG "ministers" have no cultural referents whatsoever. What would Mutesa I, a mid-nineteenth century *Kabaka* have made of a Ministry of Education and Sports, a Ministry of Health or one of Planning and Economic Development?[16] Englebert too slips from discussing what he calls "traditional resurgence" into assessing the success of the BKG as a government by its adoption of entirely new functions, particularly those involving development and democracy: "The Buganda experiment suggests, however, that it behoves traditional institutions to make the case for their revival through developmental policies, democratic practices and adaptive structures, rather than by merely calling upon the past for allegiance" (2002, 365-366). The real difficulty with using age-old culture as the rationale for government is that the underlying reason for doing so is inevitably political and the politics involved are contemporary, not "traditional". Oloka-Oyango puts this well: "... nowhere in human history has culture existed in pure and pristine separation from politics" (1997, 184). When cultural tradition becomes the servant of current political interests, it loses its claim to serve as the bedrock of government.

### Is the BKG a civil society organization?
At first glance, the BKG would seem an obvious example of an organization belonging to civil society. Before the coronation, it could only present itself as a concerned group of citizens promoting the interests of the Baganda.[17] Afterward, while its claim to be a government could be questioned, it continued to intervene energetically in the thicket of Ugandan politics to protect Baganda interests as it saw them. Even so, there are problems. Civil society is a Western philosophic concept

fashioned out of Western political collisions. It is difficult to apply in Africa because of the moral duties embedded in the concept. Indeed, in recent years, Western writers have put even greater stress on the moral obligations inherent in civil society.

In thinking about *African* civil society, this emphasis on specific norms forces us to regard civil society as an attenuated concept applying only to a few organizations—mostly those financed by Western donors, despite the rich associational life and often vocal public discourse encountered in African countries. This seems absurd. We would be much better off constructing an analysis into which we could fit organizations like the BKG. Our twin challenges then are to broaden the concept of civil society and to make it an empirical notion, leaving moral evaluation to separate, if equally important, inquiry.

In a recent analysis of civil society, Michael Edwards identifies three separate strands in prior work on civil society and suggests that they should be combined (2009, 106, 123). These approaches are civil society as associational life, as public sphere and as social formation.[18] Jointly, they represent an important advance in expressing the meaning of civil society over any one of them taken alone.[19] Thus, while civil society consists of organizations promoting particular interests, the idea also involves how those organizations express themselves and how they negotiate their positions in the larger community. Further, civil society in a particular state depends on the specific features of its social formation, including the limits imposed politically, economically and culturally on the expression and activities of local associations. Together they inform public policy and serve as a counterweight to the state—sometimes powerful, sometimes weak—without themselves competing for political power.

The problem in applying Edwards' broader conception to African civil society, however, is that he *defines* each of them normatively. In his view (and he is typical of most other current Western theorists), civil society should be understood as organizations that act morally to confront the state by helping citizens deliberate democratically and in that way contribute toward achieving the good life for all (2009, 20, 46-47, 63). To support his perspective, he invokes a multitude of attractive ideals including politeness, tolerance, inclusion, trust, truthfulness and willingness to participate in civic affairs (Edwards 2011, 7-9). Fulfillment of this notion of civil society must be left to the future—no contemporary country presents an actually existing civil society so morally driven as this ideal demands. Edwards concedes as much: "Clearly, this type of society does not exist anywhere, particularly in low-income countries, but by working backwards from this ideal it is easier to identify what can usefully be done, and when" (2011, 489).[20]

For African countries, there is more than a hint of unilinear modernization thinking going on here. But no more so than in the virtues demanded by Western analysts and donors who insist that civil society in Africa can consist *only* of those formal organizations with defined objectives that hold governments accountable while acting civilly and without compelling anyone to join (see

Chazan 1992, 281-292; Schmitter 1997, 240). Applying the moral concerns of Western assumptions about civil society would exclude most African organizations from the notion (Kasfir 1998, 4-8; Comaroff, 1999, 20-25; Neubert 2015, 12, 18). In addition, the idea of the public sphere as a Western "bourgeois" historical evolution of protected, rational and free public discussion to confront the state (Habermas 1989 [1962], 51-56, 227) seems equally alien to the ways in which shared deliberation generally occurs in African states. The latter are shaped and respond to social formations that differ considerably from those in Western countries.

Consider the societal characteristics necessary to support these Western thinkers' common notion of a civil society, a society that can support this heavy normative burden. These analysts would likely find necessary a vigorous private sector, impartial judges, a well-functioning democracy and a willingness to respect the law. To whatever degree wealthy countries in Western Europe or North America can be said to possess these characteristics, they are largely lacking in most African countries. The social formations within African countries before colonial rule, but more particularly as a result of it, have taken completely different paths. Thus, the moral baggage built into the Western notion of civil society not only leaves out most of the associations and deliberations we would want to include, it also implicitly imprints on them an unwarranted sense of moral inferiority. The fundamental problem is that African organizations ignored by the Western concept of civil society defend genuine social interests.

Several Africanist scholars have proposed a more empirical and less normative perspective on African civil society. Most of them accept the notion of civil society, but insist that we contextualize it to specific African social formations. Mahmood Mamdani reminds us that we need to understand "actually existing" African civil societies (1996, 18-21). David Lewis echoes this concern, calling for "an adaptive, historically contextualized view" (2002, 582, 578-584). Dieter Neubert argues for an even broader inclusive position for African civil society—"analyses must include all forms of self-organization" (n.d. [2015], 12). All three correctly insist that we need to trace the changes in specific African social formations to understand how members of civil society represent particular interests and engage with each other in public discourse. None of them, however, offers a satisfying argument that can support a more comprehensive and empirical framework for an African civil society that extends beyond the few organizations that qualify according to the dictates of Western theory.

Stephen Orvis takes an important step forward in creating a useful African conception by concentrating on the normative and material bases that make African organizations effective representatives for social groups. He calls attention to the additional patterns on which CSOs act beyond the liberal democratic norms that Western donors support. He further distinguishes groups organized on the basis of prebendalism (material and loyalty ties among patrons and clients) and on moral ethnicity (ethical obligations derived from ethnic group customs binding leaders and followers) (2001, 24-26).

In their different ways, he argues, these three principles set the objectives for leaders of CSOs and hold them accountable to followers. They may also overlap, as where patronage for one's ethnic compatriots is perceived as a moral obligation, while corruption, when it rewards others, is seen as a vice (2001, 26). He makes a reasonable case that these principles are evident throughout subsaharan Africa and therefore essential factors in explaining African civil society (2001, 33). His approach is empirical, because the norms he analyzes are not part of the definition of civil society. On the other hand, because he focuses solely on these norms, his analysis remains incomplete. They are part of the answer, but not in themselves sufficient to explain how African CSOs negotiate with, support or mobilize against the state.

A better framework that can serve as a foundation for conceptualizing African civil society ought to begin by empirically redefining the three approaches of civil society—associations, public sphere and social formation. Drawing from all three provides a fuller analysis of civil society more useful in Africa.[21] Associational activity has been the basis for the most common approach to civil society. Scholars who use this perspective see it as composed of the organizations that promote interests, ideologies or passions of social groups. The public sphere (or spheres) provides a second approach, analyzing the interactions and dialogue among actors engaged in discussing social issues. The focus here is on the negotiation and reconciliation of differing opinions and demands and the social spaces in which they occur. Third, the social formation offers an overarching framework that shapes who may speak, in what ways, what interests they can promote and what settlements are acceptable. Here the focus is on how the social history of a country shapes the arenas in which groups can discover what they share or how they differ.

Michael Walzer offers a commonsense framework for constructing an African civil society, one that can incorporate all three approaches.[22] For Walzer, "the words 'civil society' name the space of uncoerced human association and also the set of relational networks—formed for the sake of family, faith, interest, and ideology that fill this space" (1998, 123-24). It is his stress on "space" rather than moral criteria that makes an empirical concept possible. He makes this perfectly clear by adding, "the associational life of civil society is the actual ground where all versions of the good are worked out and tested . . . [sic] and proved to be partial, incomplete, ultimately unsatisfying. It can't be the case that living on this ground is good in itself; there isn't any other place to live" (1998, 132). In addition, by combining organizations and relational networks, he opens the opportunity to consider both associational life and the public sphere, two of the approaches necessary for analysis of African civil society.

Putting the emphasis on space also avoids two other complicating features demanded by many Western theorists. Many, perhaps most, argue that an essential feature of civil society must be the autonomy of the organizations in it (Orvis 2001, 20). The struggles for a civil society entirely independent from the one-party states in Eastern Europe in the 1980s served as an important influence on their inclusion in the contemporary notion of civil society (Keane 1998, 21-22). But complete autonomy from the state is a fantasy, because the state establishes the conditions that allow associations to function (Walzer 1998, 138). In the words of Neera Chandhoke, "the very state that civil society supposedly positions itself against, enables the latter in the sense that it provides the legal and the political settings.... The autonomy of civil society from the state emerges as an optical illusion" (2004, 150).

Orvis, on the other hand, gets into trouble by insisting on autonomy as a definitional feature. Prebendalism, one of his three normative organizing principles, depends on patrons whose connections to the state allow them to provide material benefits that sustain their groups. But if leaders are connected to the state, their groups cannot be autonomous. Patron-client groups can only be part of civil society when their leaders cannot satisfy the normative principle on which they are based! Orvis tries to rescue his argument by qualifying the extent of autonomy that groups hold without providing any basis for the qualification—"patron-client networks ... often retaining some autonomy from the state," or "Patrons' tenure within the state in Africa is often short-lived, while their position as leaders of a network of clients is much longer term" (2001, 27, 28).

Insistence on autonomy as essential to civil society deprives us of an important empirical tool. Rather than insist that CSOs must always be completely autonomous, we should think of their relations to the state as located on a continuum. There has to be some autonomy, but its extent should be a matter for empirical inquiry. At one end, accepting state regulation allows for independent associational action as well as expression in public discussion. At the other, authoritarian state control over associations and over public discussion never qualifies as civil society. Indeed, any organizations that are entirely administrative organs of the state, whether they masquerade as CSOs or not, cannot be members of civil society. Orvis is closer to the mark in his empirical observations where he qualifies the extent of autonomy than in his definition where he considers it an essential characteristic. It remains open to argument where precisely the lines separating these extremes should be drawn.

We should also qualify the idea that uncivil or involuntary organizations ought to be excluded from civil society. Here we must recognize that Walzer's use of "uncoerced" plainly introduces a normative dimension. But we need not keep that aspect of his definition. Neither Western nor African states are free from uncivil and undemocratic associations (Armony 2004; Berman 1997, 2003). Such organizations also engage in conflicts over social questions. Ethnic organizations, including religious organizations, have often been ruled outside civil society, claiming they are involuntary or uncivil (Chazan 1992, 283; Diamond 1994, 6-7). Writers who still insist that ethnicity is primordial, regard ethnic associations as potentially uncivil because they believe their members may be wholly consumed in responding to attacks on their ethnic identity. They seem to think that individuals, particularly in Africa, cannot resist ethnic organizations that make demands on the basis of descent.

But outsiders who believe in the influence of ethnic loyalty almost always exaggerate. Ethnicity by birth is ethnic, but the choice of belonging to an ethnic organization is not.

Furthermore, ethnic and religious organizations often offer benefits and promote the larger interests of their members (Chandhoke 2011, 179). An empirical notion of African civil society ought to include ethnic associations as valid members of civil society. Consequently, many ethnic associations must be seen as legitimate actors within African civil society. Still, there is a point where uncivil associations must be excluded. That point is reached with organizations that want to topple the state. If the state supplies the framework for civil society, then rebels who want either to overthrow it, or secede from it, must be understood as operating outside civil society (Walzer 1998, 138; Orvis, 2001, 20).[23]

When we ask how the public sphere operates in Africa, we need to consider it in the context of the social formations of African states. The relational networks, to use Walzer's term, that make up their public spheres are deeply affected by the disproportionate power exerted by the state over domestic organizations by comparison to Western conditions. Almost all African states emerged from colonial rule. That meant post-independent states took on the imprint of colonial autocracy (Young 2012, 336-338). Consequently, the interests and ideas of state power-holders have heavily influenced the formation of public opinion. Western-led globalization has also had enormous influence in shaping African social formations and the formation of local civil societies (Neubert n.d.

[2015], 13-17). One important result was the extensive changes to pre-colonial cultures as they came into conflict with outside influences.

While early modernization theory was wrong to assume that pre-colonial traditions would disappear, most cultural practices are no longer the customs they once were. The transformations introduced over time, some minor, others profound, are difficult to trace, particularly in the face of ardent defenses of culture. We have carefully to sort out which aspects of culture have been retained, how their meanings have changed and what their expression today actually means to those who continue to identify with them.

How do these considerations apply to the BKG? Without question, it is a highly significant actor in shaping, promoting and mobilizing Baganda interests in public discussion and governmental policy. But according to the criteria of the Western normative concept, the BKG is conclusively situated outside civil society. By definition, it is an ethnic association that claims to speak for all Baganda on the basis of birth. It expects their loyalty as its members on ethnic grounds and does not solicit members from other ethnic groups, even though it also insists on a territorial identity.[24] Its commitment to culture takes precedence over its preference for democracy or civility.

Since the principle of kingship serves as its *raison d'être*, the BKG is hierarchical in principle, although it has been open (not always successfully) to democratic decision-making. Its opposition to the government causes its opponents, the President in particular, to regard it at least on occasion as acting uncivilly. It is an odd CSO in that the political position of its cultural leader is established in the constitution. Further, the BKG seeks political power as a federal government within Uganda.

On the other hand, if we start with an empirically grounded and more expansive notion of civil society, one that combines associations, public sphere and social formation, the BKG seems an obvious candidate. It formed in 1986, years before it took its present name, to campaign for the return and then restoration of the *Kabaka*. It acts within the space between the domains of family and state to campaign for Baganda interests and royalist ideology. Because it acts for the *Kabaka*, it draws effectively on a moral ethnicity generated from widely shared cultural beliefs. It has taken on the trappings of government, although it has not been successful in achieving political power.

The BKG has productively expressed itself in the public sphere, constructing a royalist discourse that led to conflict with Museveni—part of the perils for civil society in the present Ugandan social formation. Florence Brisset-Foucault imaginatively presents a "royalist public sphere" created through the use of the Kingdom's radio station CBS "to reinvent the Buganda Kingdom" (2013, 72, 73).[25] She insightfully connects the social formation and the public sphere: "The Buganda example also shows how deliberation or discussion rules are not produced in a vacuum: they reflect power relations. Existing 'public spheres' cannot be understood without taking into account the action of the state" (2013, 85).

Paradoxically, the fact that members of several groups whom the BKG claims to represent do not think it speaks for them buttresses the case for considering the BKG a member of civil society. Like many other CSOs, it represents a restricted group with shared interests—in its case, for four reasons. First, if we think of Buganda Kingdom as occupying the borders of Buganda Region, the non-Baganda residing in it do not think of the BKG as promoting their interests most of the time. Second, many rural Baganda supported the restoration of the *Kabaka*, but prefer continued NRM rule to the initiatives of the BKG (Karlström 1999, 194-195). Third, many tenant farmers regard the BKG as representing elite landowners and not their interests. Fourth, those Baganda who felt the NRM offered a superior political program actively opposed the BKG.

But can the BKG be a CSO since it so obviously seeks power? Even though it does not aspire to replace Museveni and NRM government, it still aspires to political power. This is a substantial objection, if we work from Walzer's definition. It is fair to add that Museveni took the BKG seriously because he knew it sought political office. If the central government had adopted the CRC recommendation for federalism throughout Uganda, the BKG would have acquired office and many of the objections discussed above to its being considered a government would vanish. If that had occurred, the BKG would seem an interesting hybrid—a CSO that successfully joined political society. But that did not happen and probably will not as long as Museveni remains President.

# CONCLUSION

Ambiguities inherent in the relationship of politics to culture produced both political and conceptual collisions in the BKG's campaigns to restore Buganda's king and kingdom in Uganda. The desire of the BKG and other associations of Baganda to make Kiganda culture whole after the abolition of the monarchy resulted in restoring the *Kabaka*. But it also led to several tense political collisions during the BKG's unsuccessful pursuit of the kingdom. The peculiar position of the BKG in Ugandan politics — constitutionally prohibited, but frequently influential — poses the question of whether it makes better sense to consider it a government, part of civil society or neither. Or, whether it started out in civil society and became a government, as its officials insist.

As soon as Museveni became President, several small informal groups formed by Baganda agitated for Mutebi's return and then, having achieved that goal, successfully petitioned that he become the *Kabaka*. The BKG eclipsed the other interest groups when Mutebi chose mostly its members as his advisors. Persuading Museveni to permit kings, if only as cultural rulers, has been the BKG's greatest triumph. After that, the BKG made no progress on restoring the kingdom. It unsuccessfully opposed Museveni on several issues, sometimes resulting in severe political tensions and once in serious rioting with significant loss of life.

The issues for considering it a government differ from those for classifying it a civil society. The two problems with accepting the BKG as a government are the constitutional prohibition that forbids the *Kabaka* to exercise any powers of government and the contradictions between its cultural contentions and its cultural inheritance. Ultimately, these are political issues. The difficulties in regarding the BKG as part of civil society are conceptual. It cannot be a CSO according to the tenets of the conventional Western approach. But Western notions of civil society contain normative assumptions that exclude too much African associational activity, overlook distinctive characteristics of African public spheres and ignore the character of African social formations.

A more open empirical notion would be a far better place to start. Care must be taken to avoid replacing problematic Western concepts with problematic African-oriented notions. Nevertheless, it makes sense to locate African civil society in the space between, and to some degree overlapping, family and state. In addition to CSOs pursuing a more Western-oriented agenda, the concept should be broadened to include ethnic associations that are not necessarily democratic, nor civil, nor entirely autonomous. Furthermore, it must be understood that associations participating in African public spheres operate within specific constraints imposed by the state and by the social formations that emerged from colonialism.

Taking all these considerations into account, the BKG cannot be considered a government, but fits comfortably within an African civil society. Its capacity to succeed in some of its political demands despite the absence of any legal authority opens the way toward a more productive examination of politics in Uganda during the Museveni regime. At the same time, the BKG provides a vehicle for specifying a better basis for understanding African civil society than the conventional Western concept permits.

# ENDNOTES

1 For simplicity I call this group the BKG from 1986 forward, even though it only gained that name after the coronation in 1993.

2 Englebert insists the omission of an explicit constitutional ban on partisan political activity by the *Kabaka's* appointees gives them the right to act politically in his name (2002, 349). However, the Constitution says "a traditional leader or cultural leader shall not have or exercise any administrative, legislative or executive powers of Government or local government" (2006, ¶246(3)(f)). Uganda's courts have not yet considered this constitutional issue.

3 Mutebi concedes "even a national leader from within Buganda would find the kabakaship difficult" (Dennis 2001).

4 Oloka-Onyango speculates that "a tacit agreement" that Mutebi could come back at least as "a cultural leader" was reached when he visited liberated areas before the end of the war (Oloka-Onyango 1997, 177). Whether or not both the NRA and Mutebi saw it this way during the liberation war, it seems clear from Museveni's vacillation afterwards that he did not consider himself obligated. Rather, he was judging whether allowing Mutebi's return would improve or weaken his political position.

5 Mutebi spent several years in England and received much of his education and occupational experience there. In addition to shared cultural values, his general outlook may have been similar to the views of these young professionals.

6 Museveni seems to have decided in 1992 that it was politically necessary to return the royal properties. The previous year he had opposed their return (Karlström 1999, 237).

7 Sacralizing a fixed site as the meeting place of the *Kabaka's* officials is a significant change in Kiganda culture. Before the colonial era, the *Kabaka* and his court moved from one location in the kingdom to another.

8 Kintu Musoke, the chief government negotiator (and a Muganda) listed the properties to be returned in a letter to Museveni on 3 March 1993 (Mayiga 2009, 92). Mayiga refers to the *Lukiiko* rather than the SSC as making the decision to select a *Kabaka*. Because the 1967 Constitution had abolished the *Lukiiko*, the members of the group around Mutebi had prudently called themselves the SSC. Mayiga seems to be straining for an extra degree of legitimacy in calling it the *Lukiiko* at this time.

9 In 1975, Idi Amin's government had issued a Land Reform decree that made all land public. The decree was never implemented.

10 Local government was decentralized to the district and to its lower tiers. The central government was constitutionally obligated to supply finance, but often was slow to meet this responsibility. Federalism would have given Buganda more control over its policies as a regional government.

11 After distributing *mailo* land to the chiefs in 1900, the British Crown took control of the rest of the land in Buganda during the Protectorate period. It was "returned" to the Buganda Land Board the day before independence and transferred to the Public Land Board after the Obote government abolished the kingdom in 1967 (see Lwanga Lunyiigo 2013, 215-22).

12 The regional tier remains in the constitution, although it has not been implemented anywhere for over a decade.

13 Ironically, the pre-colonial Baganda governments did not depend on specific territorial boundaries. But taking that omission as a cultural precedent would undermine the BKG's claim to govern present-day Buganda.

14 He relies on the constitutional phrase "the institution of traditional leader ... in accordance with the culture, customs and traditions ...." (Art. 246(1)).

15 It is difficult to distinguish clearly the concepts in their analytic formulation. But on their terms, it would seem (contrary to their argument) that "institutional multiplicity" could not apply to the *Kabaka* as a "traditional" authority because his office is incorporated, "actively integrated" in their words, in the Ugandan constitution.

16 Mayiga provides a list of BKG ministries and their incumbents (2009, 155-167).

17 Looking back on this period, though, the ever-mindful Mayiga finds early indications of government in the "Kabaka's Office" created in 1986 and the "semblance of government machinery involved in setting up the Secretariat at the Ssabataka's Supreme Council in 1991" (2009, 153).

18 Instead of "social formation," Edwards calls the third approach "the good society." I restyle this notion in order to postpone any normative evaluation.

19 If civil society consists of nothing more than associational activity, we would not need two concepts (Callaghy 1994, 235-236).

20 Edwards does observe, "a forced march to civil society Western-style will do little to support the emergence of sustainable forms and norms in China, Africa, or the Middle East" (2011, 488).

21 The work needed to integrate the three approaches remains to be done. Edwards notes that his formulations remain preliminary (see 2009, 123-124).

22 Walzer offers a general framework. He does not refer specifically to African civil society. It may seem a little peculiar to rely on a Western thinker with no African expertise to find an acceptable path to a notion that fits African conditions better. However, it's the thought that clarifies that counts.

23 Neubert includes "illegal militia groups" among "all forms of self-organization" as part of African civil society (2015, 12). It is unclear whether he would exclude rebels attempting to overthrow the state.

24 One could argue that the constitution's prohibition of compulsory allegiance to any cultural leader makes the BKG a voluntary organization (Art. 246 (3)(d)).

25 She treats a specific discourse as a public sphere, suggesting that multiple public discourses in a particular society would result in multiple public spheres. It would be more parsimonious to think of the public sphere as a single space, the space created by the reach of the *de jure* state. There are conceptual issues involved in making either move.

## ACKNOWLEDGMENTS

I thank Pierre Englebert, Till Förster, Holly Hansen, Dieter Neubert, Stephen Orvis and Carol Summers for their many incisive suggestions. I am responsible for any remaining errors. I also thank Antje Daniel, Bettina Engels and Melanie Müller for inviting me to present the first version of this paper to the Workshop on Theorizing Social Movements held at the University of Bayreuth, 11 June 2014.

# REFERENCES

Armony, Ariel C. 2004. *The Dubious Link: Civic engagement and demo-cratization*. Stanford CA: Stanford University Press.

Berman, Sheri 1997. "Civil Society and the Collapse of the Weimar Republic." *World Politics,* 49:3. Pp. 401-429.

Brisset-Foucault, Florence 2013. "Re-inventing a Royalist 'Public Sphere' in Contemporary Uganda: The Example of Central Broadcasting Services (CBS)." *Journal of African Cultural Studies,* 25:1. Pp. 72-87.

Callaghy, Thomas 1994. "In Search of Civil Society." In *Civil Society and the State in Africa*. Edited by John W. Harbeson, Donald Rothchild and Naomi Chazan. Boulder, CO: Lynne Rienner. Pp. 231-253.

Chandhoke, Neera. 2004. "The 'Civil' and the 'Political' in Civil Society: The case of India." In *Civil Society in Democratization*, edited by Peter Burnell and Peter Calvert, London: Frank Cass. Pp. 143-166. Originally published in *Democratization*, 8:2 (2001).

Chazan, Naomi 1992. "Africa's Democratic Challenge." *World Policy Journal,* 9:2. Pp. 279-307.

Comaroff, John L. and Jean Comaroff 1999. "Introduction." In *Civil Society and the Political Imagination in Africa: Critical perspectives*. Edited by Comaroff and Comaroff. Chicago: University of Chicago Press. Pp. 1-43.

Constitution 2006. *Constitution of the Republic of Uganda*. Kampala.

Dennis, Ferdinand 2001. "The King and I." *Guardian* (UK). 6 October. https://www.theguardian.com/theguardian/2001/oct/06/weekend7. weekend5 (accessed 14 September 2017).

Diamond, Larry 1994. "Rethinking Civil Society: Toward democratic consolidation." *Journal of Democracy,* 5:3. Pp. 4-18.

Doornbos, Martin and Frederick Mwesigye 1995. "The New Politics of Kingmaking." In *From Chaos to Order: The politics of constitution-making in Uganda*. Edited by Holger Bernt Hansen and Michael Twaddle. Kampala: Fountain Publishers. Pp. 61-77.

Edwards, Michael 2009. *Civil Society*. Second Ed. Cambridge: Polity Press.

_____ 2011. "Introduction: Civil society and the geometry of human relations." In *The Oxford Handbook of Civil Society*. Edited by Edwards. New York: Oxford University Press. Pp. 3-14.

_____ 2011. "Conclusion: Civil society as a necessary and necessarily contested idea." In *The Oxford Handbook of Civil Society*. Edited by Edwards. New York: Oxford University Press. Pp. 480-491.

Englebert, Pierre 2002. "Born-again Buganda or the Limits of Traditional Resurgence in Africa." *Journal of Modern African Studies,* 40:3. Pp. 343-368.

Goodfellow, Tom and Stefan Lindemann 2013. "The Clash of Institutions: Traditional Authority, Conflict and the Failure of 'Hybridity' in Buganda." *Commonwealth & Comparative Politics,* 51:1. Pp. 3-26.

Habermas, Jürgen 1989. *The Structural Transformation of the Public Sphere: An inquiry into a category of bourgeois society.* Tr. Thomas Burger with the assistance of Frederick Lawrence. Cambridge, MA: MIT Press.

Karlström, Mikael 1999. "The Cultural Kingdom in Uganda: Popular Royalism and the Restoration of the Buganda Kingship." Dissertation for Doctor of Philosophy, Department of Anthropology, The University of Chicago.

Kasfir, Nelson 1976. *The Shrinking Political Arena: Participation and ethnicity in African politics, with a case study of Uganda.* Berkeley: University of California Press.

_____ 1998. "The Conventional Notion of Civil Society: A critique." *Commonwealth & Comparative Politics,* 36:2. Pp. 1-20.

_____ 2005. "Guerrillas and Civilian Participation: the National Resistance Army in Uganda, 1981-86." *Journal of Modern African Studies,* 43:2. Pp. 271-296.

Keane, John 1998. *Civil Society: Old images, new visions.* Oxford: Polity Press.

Kiwanuka, Semakula 1993. "Buganda: An ancient kingdom on the Equator." The Inaugural Coronation Lecture on the Occasion of the Royal Coronation of Ssabasajja Kabaka Ronald Muwenda Mutebi II. Kampala. 27 July.

Lewis, David 2002. "Civil Society in African Contexts: Reflections on the usefulness of a concept." *Development and Change,* 33:4. Pp. 569-586.

Lwanga Lunyiigo, Samwiri 2013. *The Struggle for Land in Buganda, 1888-2005.* Second edition. Kampala: Wavah Books.

Mayiga, Charles Peter 2009. *King on the Throne.* Kampala: Prime Time Communications.

Mazrui, Ali 1974. "The Social Origins of Ugandan Presidents: From king to peasant warrior." *Canadian Journal of African Studies,* 8:1. Pp. 3-23.

Museveni, Yoweri 2009. "Statement to the Members of Parliament on the City Riots." Parliament, Kampala. 15 September.

Neubert, Dieter n.d. [2015]. "Civil Societies in Africa? Forms of social self-organization between the poles of globalization and local socio-political order." *Bayreuth African Studies Working Papers,* No. 12.

Institute for African Studies, University of Bayreuth. Bayreuth, Germany. Originally published in German in *Leviathan*, 2011. Tr. Ruth Schubert. Pp. 185-204.

Nsibambi, Apolo Robin 2014. *National Integration in Uganda 1962-2013*. Kampala: Fountain Publishers.

Oloka-Onyango, J. 1997. "The Question of Buganda in Contemporary Ugandan Politics." *Journal of Contemporary African Studies,* 15:2. Pp. 173-189.

Orvis, Stephen 2001. "Civil Society in Africa or African Civil Society?" *Journal of Asian and African Studies,* 36:1. Pp. 17-38.

Regan, Anthony J. 1995. "Constitutional Reform and the Politics of the Constitution in Uganda: A new path to constitutionalism." In *Uganda: Landmarks in rebuilding a nation*. Edited by P. Langseth, J. Katorobo, E. Brett, J. Munene. Kampala: Fountain Publishers. Pp. 155-190.

Schmitter, Philippe C. 1997. "Civil Society East and West." In *Consolidating the Third Wave Democracies: Themes and perspectives*. Edited by Larry Diamond, Marc F. Plattner, Yun-han Chu, and Hung-mao Tien. Baltimore: The Johns Hopkins University Press. Pp. 239-262.

Walzer, Michael 1998. "The Idea of Civil Society: A path to social reconstruction." In *Community Works: The revival of civil society in America*. Edited by E.J. Dionne, Jr. Washington, D.C.: Brookings Institution Press. Pp. 123-143.

Weber, Max 1978. *Economy and Society: An outline of interpretive sociology*. Edited by Guenther Roth and Claus Wittich. Berkeley: University of California Press.

_____ 1958. "Science as a Vocation." In F*rom Max Weber: Essays in Sociology*. Edited by H.H. Gerth and C. Wright Mills. New York: Oxford University Press.

Young, Crawford 2012. *The Postcolonial State in Africa: Fifty years of independence, 1960-2010*. Madison, WI: University of Wisconsin Press.

# CARL SCHLETTWEIN LECTURES

The distinguished lecture of the Centre for African Studies Basel is held in remembrance of Dr h.c. Carl Schlettwein, who played an important part in the development of African Studies at Basel and in the establishment of our Centre. His moral support was supplemented by the generous and farsighted assistance he gave to these activities. Carl Schlettwein was born in Mecklenburg in 1925 and emigrated to South Africa in 1952. Until 1963 he lived in South West Africa, the former German colony that was then under South African administration. When he married Daniela Gsell he moved to Basel. In 1971 Schlettwein founded the Basler Afrika Bibliographien (BAB) as a library and publishing house in order to allow international institutions to access bibliographic information on South West Africa (Namibia). Accordingly, he published the first national bibliography on this African country. Through these activities the BAB contributed to documenting and researching a nation with a particularly difficult history. Other publications dealt with historical, literary and geo-methodological topics, and included titles on Swiss-African relations. From an individualistic private initiative, the BAB developed into an institution open to the public and became a cornerstone of the Centre for African Studies Basel. As the Namibia Resource

Centre—Southern Africa Library the institution is of world-wide importance. The Carl Schlettwein Stiftung, which was founded in 1994, runs the BAB and supports students and projects in Namibia as well as in other Southern African countries. In 2001, the Carl Schlettwein Foundation funded the establishment of the Chair of African History, providing the basis for today's professorship in African History and the African Studies programme at the University of Basel. The Foundation works closely with the Centre for African Studies Basel to provide support for teaching and research and in 2016 it enabled the Centre to establish a position on Namibian and Southern African Studies. The University of Basel honoured Carl Schlettwein with an honorary doctorate in 1997.

Printed in the United States
By Bookmasters